My Mother's Machine

How I became a dressmaker / designer

Gwendolyn Carr

My Mother's Machine
How I became a dressmaker / designer

© 2017 Chemical Publishing Co., Inc. All rights reserved.

No part of this publication may be reproduced, stored in a retrieval system or transmitted in any form or by any means, electronic, mechanical, photocopying, recording, scanning or otherwise, except as permitted under Sections 107 or 108 of the 1976 United States Copyright Act, without the prior written permission of the Publisher. Requests to the Publisher for permission should be addressed to the Publisher, Chemical Publishing Company, through email at:

info@chemical-publishing.com.

The publisher and the author make no representations or warranties with respect to the accuracy or completeness of the contents of this work and specifically disclaim all warranties, including without limitation, warranties of fitness for a particular purpose.

ISBN: 978-0-8206-0412-1

Chemical Publishing Company:
www.chemical-publishing.com

Printed in the United States of America

Other Books by Gwendolyn Carr

Stars and Songs
Diamonds in a Daisy Field
Legacy of Words
Prizewinning Poems and New Collections
Fierce Goodbye (in collaboration with G. Lloyd Carr)

To the memory of my dear mother
and
with gratitude to Katherine and Alyce

TABLE OF CONTENTS

1. My Mother's Machine — 9
2. Family — 12
3. The Singer Shop — 15
4. High School Decision — 17
5. Beginning — 19
6. Many Possibilities — 21
7. Challenges — 25
8. Finding Employment — 28
9. A Change — 31
10. Keep Sewing — 33
11. Buttons and Bows — 36
12. My Wedding — 39
13. Finding Customers — 42
14. Men's Clothing and Gifts — 45
15. Among the Threads — 48
16. Fashion — 51
17. An Interesting New Job — 54
18. Catastrophes — 57
19. Fame? — 60
20. What Used to Be — 62
21. Living Through It — 64
22. So You Want to Be a Dressmaker? — 66

1. MY MOTHER'S MACHINE

I begin with my mother's Singer sewing machine, because I remember it so vividly. Standing in the corner, looking as good as any other piece of furniture in the room, it was made of walnut wood, handsomely designed with two paneled front doors, and standing on four tapered legs. Opening the doors revealed a set of three drawers in one of which was a book of instructions on the care of the machine. Also a green box of attachments, which I will tell you about in a minute. Also, inside the other side was a small bracket that held the oil can, a very important item for keeping the machine in good running order. The knee lever hung down to where it could be pressed against to make the machine run. The harder one pressed it, the faster it would go. The head contained a regulator for setting the length of stitch wanted, long or short, depending on the garment being sewn and the type of fabric being used. A virtual workhorse of ingenuity, it was among the first electric Singers that boasted a lever that could be switched with the flick of a hand, for reversing the stitching without having to turn the garment around. This was the improvement of the century over the treadle machine, which needed pumping with the feet to keep it going.

Along with the purchase of the machine, Singer gave the generous offer of a series of lessons on the running of it, and the use of the various attachments for ruffling, cording, hemming of fine fabrics, the tucker, the buttonholer, the binder, the gatherer—just about everything a good homemaker would need for making the family clothing. In order to use the various attachments, we had to make something to wear. (See chapter 3.)

My mother, an excellent seamstress and embroiderer herself, had little need for more lessons, so I was to be sent to take advantage of this offer. Little did I realize where this learning was leading my life.

the next thread

2. FAMILY

Coming from a family of three girls (I was the eldest), we had the distinct advantage of a mother skilled in dressmaking and embroidery. It was natural for her to want her children to be well dressed, showing off her handiwork as well as the care of the family. Also, home sewing was much more economical than store-bought, which may need alterations to fit.

Easter meant a great deal to us—the symbolism being the shedding of heavy winter clothes and the putting on of new (usually) brighter and fancier things. A kind of resurrection. Do not submit this idea to a theologian for verification! As Easter approached we could count on whole new outfits, until we grew out of them. Generous hems, always a must, meant that our growing was followed by hems being let down. Also economical.

I well remember our tweed coats and matching hats, all of wool, for warmth in Toronto's chilly springtime. And each of us displayed a small corsage on the lapel, in honor of the break with winter.

We were always glad to leave winter behind, but that also meant leaving behind our beautiful cotton velvet dresses with crocheted collars, to be worn only on Sundays or special occasions like Christmas or a party. Along with the washing of all the family clothing was the washing of our velvet dresses. It was done on a windy day, when it was certain that the blowing would fluff out the pile. Did we ever take anything to the dry cleaners? Never!

Now into summer, mother was busy again thinking of our beach clothing. Gauzy dresses of dimity, voile, flocked material, cambric, terrycloth, or seersucker appeared as beach pajamas or floppy hats. The pajamas were similar to what we now know as a jumpsuit. All of one piece, often sleeveless, they buttoned down the front to below the waist, and the legs were flared and loose. These garments were not restrictive, but allowed us to run and jump and dig in the sand to our heart's content. It was known even then that a child left in direct sun too long would burn. Thus the floppy hat. We each sported a floppy hat, with a wide floppy brim. With the crown of white muslin (made with pie-shaped pieces), it appeared like an undulating halo.

I still have a picture of the three of us showing mother's versatility in clothing her daughters. Joanne, the youngest, has a light green dress of a soft material. The collar is a peter pan style with embroidered rosebuds at the front. The sleeves are puffed, and smocked at the lower edge, leaving a little ruffle, and smocking adorns the top of the dress, the fabric falling loosely from it. Muriel, the middle sister, sitting with her hands on her lap, shows a dress of flowered light cotton, flared, two-tiered short sleeves, and a stand-away collar, coming to a point of white voile. My dress of variable-sized elongated red checks against a white background was distinctive in that the short sleeves were flared and layered. At the waist sat a lovely black velvet belt tied in a bow at the front.

Friends sometimes scorned our homemade clothes, looking down on them, because they were not bought in a store. If they only knew that mother's workmanship was above reproach, and that "homemade" was the best made.

3. THE SINGER SHOP

The year was 1938, and I was all of ten years old. Anxious to learn sewing, I went to my first lesson at the Singer shop where all kinds of machines stood, and other students, green as I, were learning the rudiments of operating them. I'm sure the teaching and directing was extensive, but I remember the elaborate dress I finished. For a girl only ten years old, I remember that I had to deal with how to read a pattern, following it accurately to cut the fabric, and use the pins, marking where darts, pleats, and so on would be when the pattern was removed. I learned the use of the iron, scissors (use them only for fabrics, not paper dolls), the ruffler, how to baste (and why), fit, then sew the garment together, and much more. I took to it like a fish to water.

4. HIGH SCHOOL DECISION

In two years' time I entered Western Technical High School in Toronto. It was a traumatic time for the family. My mother was institutionalized as mentally unstable, and I had to learn about the intricacies of growing toward womanhood, making a decision about school, and somewhat governing my sisters when my father was at work. No such thing as after-school activities for me. I sat down with Dad and we discussed my next bit of the future. What did I want to do? Secretarial work was unappealing, woodworking, no, culinary arts, a possibility. However, since I enjoyed sewing immensely, the decision was made for me to enter Trade Dressmaking. In fact, the only subjects I truly cared about were art, English, and dressmaking. The rest—science, geography, history, book-keeping, etc.—were only to be tolerated. Sewing was the big adventure. I realize now that writing, art, and sewing have an affinity with each other. To make something out of existing materials (paint, fabric, words) is a way to use one's creative side. And technical school was the place to do it. And mother's machine was now mine!

the next thread

5. BEGINNING

The sewing room was our sanctuary. Miss Lindsay, a mild-mannered, patient, and kind matron was to be our teacher, and she devoted her life to our future as fine seamstresses, knowledgeable in their profession and ready to use their knowledge in the world of fashion. You may wonder at this, but in my day women teachers were unmarried. Once they became Mrs. they lost their employment with the classroom.

Because our class was comprised of only six students, we had the distinct advantage of close attention by Miss Lindsay. Deliberately, and quietly, we were instructed in the best habits of the craft, and always corrected with gentle persuasion until we got it "right." The primary rule for any seamstress was that she wear a thimble on the middle finger of the right hand. Why? This metal, mushroom-like tool was used to push the needle through the fabric. The tougher the fabric, the harder you had to push. Canvas, leather, or heavy jean material necessitated a good push, until, thankfully, the needle appeared on the other side. And then you pull. Here, I am speaking about hand sewing. This little maneuver with the thimble meant that your finger was spared the pain of having a hole punched in it through years of sewing. Often defying the teacher's admonition when she wasn't looking, we soon came to realize that the hole could become infected. Lesson learned!

the next thread

6. MANY POSSIBILITIES

What kinds of materials did we students work with? Fabrics: wool, cotton, silk, rayon, linen, velvets of cotton, linen, or silk, lamé, voile. Then there was leather, straw, and suede for hat and glove making. Not all fabrics are cooperative under the machine needle. Some stretched or puckered, and were sleazy and hard to control. Learning the properties of each of these materials, we could deal with them accordingly. Cotton, linen, wool, and rayon were the most amenable to dress or suit making, and gave little resistance to management.

What other kinds of sewing did we learn? Smocking became part of our training. Many children owned a smocked dress for wear on Sunday, and for special occasions. Smocking is a type of embroidery where the fabric is gathered tightly on an already-printed dot pattern. With colored embroidery threads, the dots were followed in various patterns, embellished with French knots. With the making of a cluster of such knots, a flower could be created. This encounter with smocking in school reminded me of the dress my mother made me when I was young. The fabric itself was dotted, Swiss, lightweight, red with white tiny dots. Mother was so adept at smocking that she worked it freehand, without a printed pattern to go by. The finished dress then was smocked in white from the neck to the waistline, and I could wear it with pride in mother's fine work.

Hand-stitched gloves were on the curriculum as one of the skills to be learned. Made of very supple kidskin, the many pieces had to fit our own hands precisely. This was very time-consuming, but the end results gratifying, as each of us had a classy pair of gloves to be worn with a suit (and hopefully, not lost somewhere).

Then we made hats. Hats were worn frequently in our day to set off our particular outfit, or to frame our face. We always went out "dressed." Hat, gloves, and dress—the complete outfit for a young girl or lady. Hat forms, always available at our favorite store, could be covered with straw by the yard, or fabric to mix or match with a dress. When we completed the body of the hat, it was back to the store of endless variety in order to find just the right kind of decoration to finish it. Would it need a ribbon, braid, feathers, a buckle, or a single, beautiful silk flower? It was hard to decide.

More mundane, but essential for learning dressmaking from the bottom up, was the making of a pattern from construction paper. This is called drafting. I can't tell you much about this part of my education, because I did not pay proper attention to it, preferring in the future to buy good Vogue patterns from the catalogue for making my wardrobe. Just another excuse to make my way to the fabric shop, and browse. This was not just an idle way of passing time, but it became a time of learning and instruction—the extended classroom, you might say. Gazing at and examining various fabrics was a way of familiarizing oneself with weaves and textures, weights and patterns, so that when contemplating the making of something, you would know what was suitable for the project.

Also, one became adept at discerning silk from polyester, wool from nylon, rayon from cotton, pure linen from a linen mix, without referring to the label on the bolt or roll, which contained the price per yard and the content of the fabric.

A knowledge of weaves is important to know when making anything. Generally, the tighter weaves are sturdier, and longer wearing, while a loose weave has room to move as the threads scrape against one another. Some weaves are known as twill, plain, jacquard, damask, satin, or herringbone. Design (flowers, stripes, checks, etc.) has always been important to me. Cheaper materials usually have inferior colors and designs. Not so the better fabrics, which you can tell by more pleasing design and color. Looking at good fabrics long enough, one acquires an instinct for the best. Yes, they are more costly. "You get what you pay for" is still true.

the next thread

7. CHALLENGES

My big one came when Miss Lindsay informed us that it was now time to learn "in real life." We were to make a dress for someone—mother, aunt, friend, or neighbor. The other girls chose their mother because she would be at home, handy for fitting and consulting if she required changes. Since my mother was now away from home, I chose Miss Abernethy, our school's Culinary Arts teacher. She was very agreeable to this, and proceeded to buy her own material and pattern. She was tall and gaunt, on the order of Abraham Lincoln, mild and easy in temperament. One part of this challenge was her chosen material. A dress crepe, known for "hanging" and draping, was not very stable under the sewing-machine needle. A hard-to-manage fabric was mine to work on.

I had proceeded to cut it out and baste it together, ready for a preliminary fitting, when Miss Abernethy's mother died. Having to attend to the funeral arrangements and grieving over the loss, she took some time before returning to school. By the time she did, many pounds had been lost from her already thin frame. It was with trepidation that I now had to work with a basic skeleton, refitting something that hung like a sack on a stick. She patiently stood while I employed pins by the dozen, taking in inches of material, then rebasting, refitting, until the dress was true to her form. The term "alteration" was foreign to me then, but that is exactly what I was doing.

The last project was the making of our graduation dresses, which, as Miss Lindsay explained, were to be street-length, practical, but of good material, and smart. Nothing like today's fancy, off-the-shoulder, glitzy gowns, these were pretty ordinary dresses, made well and of very good material.

I chose a very fine, lightweight fabric of 50 percent cotton and 50 percent wool, known by the trade name of Viyella. My wardrobe, always ready to accept its favorite color, chose pale blue. With short raglan sleeves the dress had an inset band at the waist, a casually gathered skirt, and a bodice with an interesting banded neckline. Nothing extreme. The neckline boasted a tab with a single expensive silver button designed like a knot. This highlight of the dress, important to any dressmaker who values the distinction of a good button, I spent some time in choosing it. Adornment can be overdone!

the next thread

8. FINDING EMPLOYMENT

Graduation came and went. Now what? I was sixteen years old and facing the prospect of finding a job. Very shy, and reluctant to look for employment, I nevertheless did. The year was 1944, and the place to look was the newspaper. Running down the wanted column, I spied an advertisement for seamstress at the shop of Marie Cluthé, an exclusive French establishment dealing in wedding gowns. Yonge Street in Toronto was like Newbury Street in Boston, replete with shops selling expensive goods, boutiques, and small, extravagant places to eat. This is where I was to go for an interview, bringing my high school diploma as proof of my capabilities in Trade Dressmaking. And so it was that I entered that French establishment, past the elegantly dressed window with the single bride in her gorgeous wedding gown.

Was I ready for this? The pleasant lady who interviewed me explained my duties, which were to help the head dressmaker with gowns that needed minor alterations. Salary? Five dollars a week. I was fortunate to catch this job right out of high school. Always prompt (an asset), I took my place at the table in these light and amiable surroundings, and set to work. I was only employed there for a few weeks, as my father thought the pay was too little, and advised me to quit. In obedience to him, I sadly left the luxurious shop, the Yonge Street atmosphere, and what might have become a career in couture fashion. I quickly found work in a furrier's on Spadina Avenue. Not a fashionable street, it was nevertheless lined with other businesses that dealt in clothing, similar to New York's garment district.

The advertisement was clear enough. "Girls wanted to hand-sew lining into fur coats." The money offered was better, and I always enjoyed hand sewing, being good at it, and quick. I was hired, and began.

Chinchilla, beaver, muskrat, lamb's wool, and mink comprised the inventory the seamstresses worked on. Coats made of these various furs were put together by furriers skilled at piecing the skins and sewing them to make a coat. This work was done in another room, and when the outer coat was completed, the big boss of our room brought us a coat along with a lining, which we sewed in by hand.

As we sat "finishing" the coats, we talked among ourselves, aware that our boss kept up a constant stroll around the room, always smoking a cigar and lighting one from another. The chatter was peppered with lots of advice for me, the youngest in the room. The Ukrainian woman thought she wanted me for her daughter-in-law, and sometime soon would introduce me to her son. But she would have to find another prospect, because after some months I decided to look elsewhere for work.

the next thread

9. A CHANGE

Going into factory work in a large Canadian company would develop me in many ways. As a shy young person with little experience of the wider world, I encountered many types of humanity employed in this place: the woman who swore like a trooper and was running around with her married section boss; the lonesome, mild man who took a shine to me, bringing the token of a turkey and cranberry sauce sandwich every Thanksgiving; the employee whose wife had contracted cancer and confided concern over the fact that his house could be taken in order to pay the bills. Each personality was evident as I worked at my job for seven years in noise and heat, around machinery that one took care not to get too close to. Always respect moving objects!

My section boss, also a cigar smoker, was kind and considerate, so much so that he thought to introduce me to a group of five girls that he thought I might have something in common with. I was to enjoy their company for many years, making close friendships that I managed to stay in touch with after I moved away.

Although the thought of becoming a writer never occurred to me at that time, I contributed to the company's newspaper with a small column titled "Christian's Corner," which contained a few thoughts on a verse of scripture. One woman who worked alongside of me consistently ridiculed my faith, but I was able to take it and stand firm.

This factory gave me excellent pay, which I very much needed in light of the fact that my marriage was coming soon. Money was scarce in the family, necessitating my having enough to pay for all wedding expenses myself.

the next thread

10. KEEP SEWING

Through seven years of factory work, I never lost sight of the fact that I was still a dressmaker with the intent of pursuing that profession. Evening hours and Saturdays still left time for sewing projects. New pillows for the sofa, a pad for the chair, curtains, a new bedspread, and always a new dress for dating.

The decorating urge often called me to do some refurbishing, whether or not rooms needed updating. Always devising ways to add a little something here or there, I found that fabric shops were a constant temptation. And I usually gave in to it. Anxious to see what the latest was in the way of fabrics, I found myself inside the shop, and browsing. Remnants, lying innocently in bins, were the first to be looked at. Couldn't something fashionable be made out of that bright print? Take it home anyway. Something will come up.

Saturdays were excellent days for taking a trip to Toronto's Chinatown. Always savoring the experience of entering another culture, I walked along streets lined with shops full of pastries, whole ducks strung up by their legs, blue and white rice bowls and china spoons or chopsticks, the fragrance of sweet-and-sour sauces emanating from open doors. Just one more temptation before reaching the fabric shops.

Tables and shelves full of a large variety of fabrics greet the woman looking for cloth. The browsing business is good here. They don't care how long you stay, or how much you buy, or how many questions you ask about the properties of certain goods. I'm here to stay a while.

Most shops had a basement where remnants galore enticed the frugal buyer. The basement held many other notions having to do with stitching, odd bits of this and that, discontinued merchandise, etc.; budget-wise women usually started here. I did. The remnants were usually large enough to make a dress or suit. Finding a piece of fine suiting (men's or women's) would make my day.

Silks, of course, were the specialty in Chinatown, coming as they did from the other side of the world. The wonderful thing about silk is that it takes the dye like no other fabric, producing the most gorgeous colors and sheen.

Miss Lindsay had taught us well on the unique properties of each fabric, and what to expect in the finished product. And I learned by experience. She was a great teacher.

The year Ultra Suede came to the market, I thought a coat made of it would be dashing. With pattern in hand, I went shopping for a piece of wine-colored suede, brought it home, cut it out, put the internal stiffening in the lapels, down the front, in the pocket flaps, lined it, made the buttonholes, and sewed the buttons on. Then one cold day I went walking in that coat. I came to a sober conclusion: as good as it looked, it had NO warmth in it whatever. Lesson learned.

the next thread

11. BUTTONS AND BOWS

A seamstress's paradise, located in downtown Toronto, was a mere slot-in-the-wall of a shop. A narrow edifice of brick, it held everything in the way of notions that one could want or dream of. From floor to ceiling, box upon box, drawer upon drawer, it held an unbelievable assortment of buttons, ribbon, braid, buckles, beads, elastic, needles, pins, embroidery hoops, feathers, snaps, hooks, silk flowers, straw braid, veiling, hat forms, cording, and whatever else I've forgotten to tell you about.

If you were interested in an item near the ceiling, that was okay too. A salesperson would climb a rolling ladder, and with a smile, show you the box of whatever it was you wanted.

Time spent there was time well spent, as ideas for "making" came tumbling out. I never wanted to leave until I had seen just about everything. Did I mention the name of that shop? It was called the Button Shop, and that was an understatement!

These forays into the Button Shop remind me of the dress I made for my sister's wedding. It was of pale pink, finely corded faille, a fitted bodice and slim short skirt. It featured a fishtail peplum, a six-inch overskirt from the waist, extending to the back of the dress in a fishtail or point. I banded the edge of the peplum with a one-inch silver lamé trim, and treated the sleeves in the same way. And yes, that lovely silver lamé set the dress off, thanks to the Button Shop.

Being practical by nature, I made what was good for not only one occasion, but many. I wore that particular dress to parties, at New Year's and Christmas. It always looked elegant.

One more note about practicality: every piece of fabric I bought was hand washable. As we were instructed to do in class, after the material is purchased, submit it to water. If it shrinks, it will do so now. No worries about it shrinking after the garment is made. The one exception to this rule was the fabric for my wedding gown.

the next thread

12. MY WEDDING

With my own September wedding coming soon, my mind was on "the dress." What should it be? Of course I would make it, and at a fraction of the price of a store-bought. For the modest price of fifty dollars, a heavy cream satin was chosen for the underdress, and French lace over it. Long, slender sleeves, pointed at the wrist, were closed with several small covered buttons. The bodice was fitted with a peter pan collar, and a row of covered buttons from the neckline to the waistline in the center. The full long skirt was so shaped as to extend into a short train at the back. The overall look was of an expensive gown that fit well.

Then what to wear for going away on the honeymoon? In considering the autumn weather, I wondered what would be appropriate for color. My choice was a dark, vibrant shade of turquoise for the dress, and rust-colored snakeskin purse and shoes. Gloves were of rust fabric with beading. The fabric would of course have to be silk (back to Chinatown). I bought a shantung, which is a raw silk with a slub. The style was short-sleeved, a fitted bodice, and the neckline basically square, but with two peaks at the bottom of the square. Three large covered buttons closed the bodice front. The skirt was gored and flared with a wide belt, the covered buckle of which was diamond shaped, echoing the neckline.

With the making of my own dresses, the busyness increased. I came up with the brilliant idea of overlapping leaves for the bridesmaids' headpieces. Consequently, I wanted to make them of the same silk as their dresses. The maid of honor in rust, and the two bridesmaids in turquoise, their headbands would match. Each band was composed of seven wired leaves, covered in silk, with a border of bugle beads along the edges. This was time-consuming handwork, but the result was unusually beautiful. Our photographer thoughtfully took a picture of the bridesmaids looking down on my ring as we sat on a sofa. The headbands show clearly.

The year 1953 was exceptionally busy, and exceptionally hot. Hoping to avoid summer heat, we planned a fall wedding in September. But relentlessly, that heat followed us all the way to New York and Washington.

Among the many historical sights, monuments, and other places of interest, we inevitably visited museums. My instinct for fabrics, on full alert as we toured through rooms hung with lush draperies, kept me hanging back from the docent to better inspect the fringes and damasks. Hard not to touch. Those guards keep a steely eye out for anyone getting too close. Nevertheless, I took in the upholstery and fine fabrics on the French chairs and sofas, and noticed their impeccable workmanship. Seams looking seamless, patterns matching exactly, reinforced what Miss Lindsay had taught us in school about doing things well. It is true that what I saw in the museum was the best in regard to fabrics, but even plain cotton coverings look better if they are well made. Workmanship is important.

the next thread

13. FINDING CUSTOMERS

As a dressmaker just beginning to gather customers, most of which was done by word of mouth, I was pleased to get a call from a woman wanting a dress for New Year's dancing and festivities. The smart little black dress, always in style, was what she wanted. She went on to explain that as a professional model in England, she had quit because of the men pinching her derriere. She was tired of it. I assumed she was used to high fashion, and that proved right, as she knew exactly what style she wanted, so needed no guidance from me. Very pleasant to deal with, and grateful too, as the compliments swirled around her when she wore it. She was thoughtful enough to phone me next morning to report what a hit the dress had made.

A satisfied customer is a good customer.

At this time I was a new mother, convinced that working from home was a wise alternative to working for someone else. The skills I had went with me, along with my mother's machine. But of course, my toddler always went with me too, and jealous of my attention to the bridesmaid's gown currently being worked on, he would tug at it as it moved off the machine. Not good. I became a worker on the night shift. Getting him in bed early became my goal. Lots of sleep for good health was the motto of the day.

Making boys' clothes is not nearly as exciting as designing frills and flounces for a little girl, but a dressmaker's son ought to be well dressed also. Two outfits stand out in my mind. When he was two, and it was nearing Easter, my machine busied itself making him a soft light blue wool coat and hat. Being overly ambitious, I made myself a lovely grey dress and matching jacket. Also a straw hat. Easter, being important to us, meant that new clothes were a symbol of Christ's resurrection, in that the old wardrobe was past, and something new and bright made one's body feel more alive. Do not ask a theologian to verify that!

the next thread

14. MEN'S CLOTHING AND GIFTS

This detour into boys' clothing extended to my husband also. Feeling extra charitable or overconfident of my abilities, I offered to make him a jacket that he could wear in the classroom, when teaching his college students. He accepted this offer gladly. Of a plain woven, soft wool, in an unusual shade of wine, it boasted all the tailoring bits and pieces that a man's jacket has: the inside welt pocket, the outer flap pockets, pointed lapels, sleeve vents with the required four buttons, and hand-sewn heavy satin lining. One dark-wine unique button closed the jacket. Through many compliments he wore it and wore it, and to this day will not throw it out.

And when our son married, he too wanted a suit in which to take his vows. Launching out again into waters that my school training had not prepared me for (tailoring is a wholly different thing), I proceeded to make the navy blue cotton velvet of his choice, and a red cummerbund to show it off. Since men's clothing is highly constructed with inner stiffenings and impeccable tailoring, this effort was a labor of love.

Over the years, the making of Christmas gifts has always been a good challenge to my creativity, and I rise to the occasion with something that I think friends and family would like. One year I took lessons in fabric stenciling, which necessitated using inks that would withstand washing, a stubby brush for pounding in the inks, and waxed patterns that were either made or bought. My ambition was to make ties for the men in my life. Not satisfied with the bought patterns, I composed my own designs onto heavy waxed paper. At this time we lived in the home of an old gentleman who gardened for people on a nearby estate. Since he was a little lax in caring for his personal appearance, I thought he ought to have at least one good tie. Come Christmas, he was greatly surprised and pleased to get a uniquely handmade tie. This gave him, upon wearing it, occasions to brag about who had made such a wonderful creation. As time went on, this was the only tie he would wear, and I noticed it was becoming quite soiled, so I took it from him one day and gently washed and ironed it, returning it to him. I doubt if he ever threw it out. Other friends received placemats for the table, fringed and stenciled with my own designs or their initials in the corner.

Then there was the year of vest making. One for my husband, and one for his dad. They were made of a muted tartan Viyella, and therefore washable. Each one made with loving care and hours of work, they were received with gratitude, and worn for years. Did you know that a simple vest has seventeen pieces of pattern to cut out and assemble? Think, before you try it!

the next thread

15. AMONG THE THREADS

Some things learned along the way: all fabrics are not equal, but have minds of their own. Closely woven fabrics are stable and long wearing. A bedsheet with a high count of threads per inch is better than one with a lower count. And that nubby material that is so attractive is loosely woven, the spaces in between an invitation for the threads to scrape against one another, thus wearing the cloth out in no time. A loose weave is prone to getting caught on furniture, bobby pins, brooches, or anything else you might be in contact with that is rough. It will snag a loop, and pull the thread into a pucker. Sleazy and stretchy fabrics have their own negative qualities, so one must be prepared to deal with them, or not use them at all.

The most cooperative materials are cotton, wool, linen, rayon, and silk. I've learned that the headaches are fewer if I use the most cooperative. Most anything can be made with this array of fine fabrics: curtains, drapes, pillows, book covers, swags, tablecloths, cornices, scarves, bathing suits, coats, jackets, lamp shades, dresses, or anything else that catches your fancy.

When buying material for any project, several things need to be considered. Design and color are often the first things that draw, but they are not the best. More important is the kind of article you want to make. A sturdy bag or pair of jeans, a flimsy piece of lingerie, a stretchy bathing suit, a glitzy evening skirt, placemats, and so on. The fabric is important to the use. Do I need to consider washability, creaseability, warmth, coolness? Can I wear it to Italy or the Arctic? Does it need special care? These questions should be asked before money is paid out for good material on which long hours of labor will be spent.

Another thing learned along the way: be prepared! A dressmaker's reputation follows her. With friends clamoring for her certain skills, she is drawn into a variety of enterprises. And so it was that the opportunity came to design and make costumes for two of Charles Williams' morality plays that my husband was directing at college. The personality of each character would be reflected in the costumes' color and design. This was my assigned job. A new venture. Character, fabric, design of costume, and cost were all to be considered in that big project. Geometric blocks of bright primary colors were chosen for the players, and worked well, giving the desired effect.

One's skill in working on clothing, or interior items for the homes of the wealthy, was always welcomed. But I remembered those whose needs were more modest. Within walking distance of our home there was a residence for elderly ladies. They no longer sewed and hoped to find someone who would mend that favorite nightgown, or insert new elastic in their underwear, and reinforce the closures on their bras. They still had pride in keeping their clothes in "good repair." A time was set for me to visit two friends that lived together in the home, and as I set foot in the hallway, a whispering of "the dressmaker is here" came to greet me. I had a great time with these ladies, and they were appreciative of my services, and the fact that I came over to them, collected the clothing, and delivered it back to them. I was glad for "small things."

the next thread

16. FASHION

"What's the latest fashion?" many ask as they refurbish their wardrobe. No matter what it is, they wear it without a thought as to whether or not it might flatter their particular shape. Fashions come and go, and you won't look good in them all. By all means, try on various styles in the store, but notice how each one makes you look. Does it work well with your frame, your coloring? Does it accent what you want to minimize? Taking into account your budget, will it last more than a season or two? Buying basics like navy, grey, black or brown, is practical and smart. Then you use brighter colors in scarves, blouses, and other accessories that complement the basics and complete your outfit. Tight clothing does nothing for you. Avoid it.

The classics are always in vogue, whereas the extremes of trendy styles are here today, and gone tomorrow. Case in point. A long-time friend of mine, living in another state, called me one day, saying she had a coat from college days that she loved, and wanted to keep wearing. She was now fifty-five. This coat, a winter-weight wool, houndstooth Pendleton was still good, but the lining was in shreds. Could I reline it? Of course. It arrived by mail shortly after our conversation. Unpacking it, and inspecting it thoroughly for worn spots, I was surprised that there were none. The wool, after thirty years' wear, was still intact, and the style still in vogue. But the lining was literally in ribbons. Carefully removing it, and taking each section apart, I bought a good dress crepe and proceeded to place the old onto the new, cutting it out, pinning, then basting and sewing the pieces together. This then went into the coat by hand, the body first, the sleeves next, then the hem. This project turned out well, but was especially hard for me working on the black lining. I had lost the sight of my right eye the year before, and it became difficult to work on black. It absorbs the light.

"Change it." The most joyful part of being a seamstress/designer comes when a customer says, "I don't like the collar, the shape of the sleeves, the fullness of the skirt, the way the neckline sags, the slit in the back. Can you change it?" Those very words are like dessert to me—delicious! All my creative juices are stirred just thinking about the possibilities. What don't you like? What can be done about it? Suggestions are always welcome, because usually they don't have any. It is alteration and redesigning all in one. Personally, I change literally everything I buy, even if it is no more than changing the buttons. I keep a stash in a tin right beside my mother's machine.

the next thread

17. AN INTERESTING NEW JOB

Our move to New England necessitated my finding employment, getting established, and finding new customers for alteration work. Gradually, things fell into place, as our son settled in a new school and made a few friends. Soon, I was to hear of need for a sew-er at an upholstery establishment that had been in business for a long time, doing work for the wealthy people of the North Shore and Boston. Given their desire for the very best, only fabrics of high quality were used. It was into this environment that I was hired. From the refined dressmaking I had been doing, I was now introduced to the heavier, more elaborate upholstery and drape materials that I would be working with. This was interior home furnishing, which included the use of English chintz, brocade, damask, sturdy cotton, linen, silk, or cotton velvets. With fabrics heavy enough to withstand the wear and tear of sitting, this was a world away from the small prices of dress materials to twenty- or thirty-dollar-a-yard fabric. I became used to high-quality goods, and it wasn't hard.

This foray into seven years of watching and learning a bit of the trade added to my repertoire as seamstress. The one difference was that I worked on a large commercial Singer that took large spools of thread and handled very heavy fabrics. The upholstery was handled by the boss, while I sewed the slip-covers, pillows, and drapes. The cutting and pinning of the slip-cover was the boss's job; then he handed it to me along with strips of bias material, which covered the cording for the edges of cushions and sofa. The bias strips were done first, sewn together in one long snake that was then used to cover the cording. Some large sofa cushions were to be filled with down, and I was interested to learn the making of the inner casing for these cushions. Made of very tightly woven (down-proof) cotton, the cushions needed to have channels or walls put in them so as to keep the feathers from shifting. In each channel, a small opening was left in which the down was blown by machine.

It was hard work slinging a large sofa cover around on the machine, but in the process, observation and familiarity with this type of sewing helped me learn a different skill. I finally thought I could make a slip-cover for my sofa at home. So I ordered the required number of yards of Federal blue cotton velvet, semi-confident that I could do this. Taking it home on a big roll, I put it in the living room, and left it there a few weeks before mustering up the courage to cut into it. But the day inevitably came. With the boss's admonition ringing in my ear "Measure twice, cut once" I took the plunge, with this revision. Measure twice, PRAY, cut once. It was scary, but diligent to the end, I did accomplish the making of the slip-cover. I have since made sheer curtains, chintz drapes, pillows, and cornices for myself and others. Decorating is one of the most exciting things to do. I love the decision-making that goes into changing a room. Dealing with color, texture, and design is right up my alley, and just plain fun!

18. CATASTROPHES

One of my steady customers who had been coming to me for years bought a colored striped jacket that needed the sleeves shortened. There was an intricate trim at the wrist, and in the course of removing it, I cut a gash into the sleeve proper. Extremely upset, I immediately called the lady, explaining what happened. She was very calm, and said that since the jacket was this season's, there may be a chance of getting some material from the cutting table of the manufacturer to replace the sleeve. She called the store, explaining the situation, and they immediately called the manufacturer, and sure enough, they retrieved a yard of fabric, and sent it right out to me. You can imagine my relief that this catastrophe turned out so well, and that my customer was so casual about the whole incident.

With some disbelief, I unfold the following story. Another longstanding customer phoned me one day not long after I had done an alteration on her husband's jacket. "Gwen, do you have a small pair of scissors missing?" "Well, Joan, I have a half dozen or so small scissors, and I wouldn't realize it if one pair were missing," I explained. "Why do you ask?" "I think you left a pair in John's jacket, and he is afraid to sit down for fear of stabbing himself." I could not believe what I was hearing. When she brought the jacket back to me, and I opened the lining, there they were. To this day, I don't believe I ever did such a thing. But what about a doctor who leaves an item in a patient? Unsolved mysteries.

Then there is the mistake of mismeasuring, especially when making curtains. I sometimes excel at this particular fault, but usually on my own goods.

Once in a while, I would cut the fabric too short! I am adept at rectifying this situation, by purchasing a coordinating material in order to make a border, and tie-backs to match. No one would know that I had not planned it that way.

the next thread

19. FAME?

In my corner of New England, there was a famous dress shop called Ina's: "Ina's of New York, Palm Beach, and Magnolia." Situated in a residential area, it was well known to those used to purchasing good clothes, and customers would drive a distance to this small town in order to do so. Here, one could find a ball gown, fine suit, dressy dress, cruise-wear, a hat and shoes to match. It was a thriving concern and I was fortunate enough to do alterations for them. Since many dresses were filmy, fragile concoctions, of sometimes many layers, they were nerve-wracking to alter. Ina finally retired, and sold the business to Louise. As a new owner, she tried some innovative things to attract customers. The store boasted a grand piano, and Louise's husband came to the shop on certain days to play some of the old tunes familiar to most people. Who wouldn't stay long enough to hear the music, browsing all the time, and probably making a purchase in the end? Come springtime, Louise gathered a few girls together, and put on a fashion show to advertise the newest pieces of clothing the store would carry. Of course, none of us were professionals, but with a little coaching on how to walk, twirl, open the coat to show the lining or the dress, we found that the experience was so much fun. Yes, I was part of the group, and that was part of my life. The fashion business.

the next thread

20. WHAT USED TO BE

Over the span of the last forty years, Boston and surrounding towns have changed greatly. New housing, businesses, parks, people, and fashions changed. I noticed it. Though we all encourage change, we pine for the loss of the familiar, or what used to be. Arriving from Toronto in the early sixties, I immediately explored a wide area for fabric stores, checking on which ones sold what kinds of goods. Several large establishments displayed an extensive variety of fabrics, and there were the little shops with exclusive silks and wools from Italy or Britain. There was also the matter of trims and buttons. Where did one find a wide selection? What about down and other fillings for pillow-making? Soon I learned, and kept track of who sold what. Inevitably, and one by one, fabric stores were closing. Women, now going to business or/and buying store-boughts, no longer sewed. But I had customers, and required at least the essentials, like threads and buttons, linings, needles, and pins. Have you tried shopping for a needle lately?

The very last bastion for seamstresses was Boston's Chinatown. Going by train, this was my last hope of finding worthy fabric for projects I wanted to do. But, over time, these shops too closed their doors. The only place left now is New York City, which is totally inconvenient for me as a place to shop and still be home for supper. Only on occasions when my husband and I plan a special trip for other reasons (like the opera) do I walk along the garment district on Seventh Avenue, lapping up the dazzling array of bolts and bolts of gorgeous materials, and I feel like the fashion business is still in business. Everything is there, ready to be made into "something." I usually succumb.

21. LIVING THROUGH IT

If you live long enough, you have seen everything. In the world of fashion I have lived through hoop-skirts, straight skirts, minis, the new look, the pencil, the slit, the dirndl, tie-dyed whatever, the flounce, puff sleeves, no sleeves, kick pleat, inverted pleat, and the un-hemmed. Have I missed anything? Each has had its day in the sun, and will do so again.

I began this strand of my life becoming acquainted with my mother's machine, taking lessons at the Singer machine shop, then entering high school for a four-year course in Trade Dressmaking. I continued making my livelihood with those skills. This satisfied my creative bent, not only with various other kinds of materials, but with fabrics and fashion.

Ironically, my mother was institutionalized just when I entered high school, and she never came out of the asylum. She never knew of my ongoing abilities, or what I did with them. But as I sit at my machine, thoughts of her arise, and leave me wondering if she would be proud to know how well her machine was used. It has been a true friend that has served me well. A workhorse that is always there, ready to go whenever I want it to. Morning or night, when sleep avoids me, it woos me with garments waiting to be repaired, altered, or newly made. It is willing to do them all. Over seventy-two years, and still running.

the next thread

22. SO YOU WANT TO BE A DRESSMAKER?

1. What are the advantages?

You are not at the mercy of commercially made clothing, but can make whatever you desire, and what suits you. This can develop into a business, done from home, and on your time.

2. What is the best advertisement for your work?

Your impeccable workmanship and care taken with your customers to make the garment fit well.

Word of mouth is always reliable.

Having business cards printed is inexpensive, and they can be given to existing customers to pass on.

3. What do you need to get started in business?

Good tools: a machine that works properly, because you remember to oil it.

A space big enough to handle fabrics, ironing board, spools of thread, a place to hang finished or in-progress work.

Paper, pencil, ruler, tape measure, ripper, good scissors for use on fabrics ONLY.

Adequate light.

Organization. Keep a calendar for making appointments. Mark the date for customer pick-up. If they insist on a final fitting at this time, do it, but if the original fitting was accurate, the garment should be okay. It will be understood that payment is expected at pick-up. Always let your customer know that if anything is not as it should be, they should say so, and it can be rectified.

4. Is it proper to make suggestions to a customer?

Of course, especially if they do not know what they want, or if what they want cannot be done at all. If a customer is definite about how something should look, do not argue. They assume the outcome of their own decisions.

5. Some questions you may ask yourself:

Is my interest in working with fabrics high enough to make it a life work?

Am I good with my hands?

Do I have an eye for fashion, a liking for people, an insistence on perfection, and the satisfaction of the customer?

Do I take criticism badly, or do I learn from it?

When doing alterations, will the garment look better when it leaves my house than when it came in?

Are you willing to give an honest appraisal to someone who comes to you wanting to know if the dress suits them, or not?